Managing Editor
Mara Ellen Guckian

Editor in Chief
Karen J. Goldfluss, M.S. Ed.

Creative Director
Sarah M. Smith

Cover Artist
Barb Lorseyedi

Illustrator
Kelly McMahon

Art Coordinator
Renée Mc Elwee

Imaging
Craig Gunnell
James Edward Grace

Publisher
Mary D. Smith, M.S. Ed.

WITHDRAWN

Author
Tracie Heskett, M.Ed.

For correlations to the Common Core State Standards, see page 7.
Correlations can also be found at
http://www.teachercreated.com/standards

Teacher Created Resources
6421 Industry Way
Westminster, CA 92683
www.teachercreated.com

ISBN: 978-1...

© 2014 Teacher
Made i...

D1157856

Teacher Created Resources

Table of Contents

Introduction

The *Healthy Habits for Healthy Kids* series was created to provide educators and parents with simple activities that help students learn to make healthy food choices, appreciate the importance of daily exercise, and develop healthy habits they will maintain throughout their lifetimes. Students who are healthy are better able to learn and be successful.

The activities in this book help students understand where the foods they eat come from and why nutritious food choices are beneficial to them. The objectives outlined by the USDA Food Guidance System (*ChooseMyPlate.gov*) formed the foundation upon which the activities in this book are based. Each of the five food groups is explored in depth. The goal is to build an understanding of the need to incorporate fruits, vegetables, whole grains, protein, and dairy into our daily diet. Students will also explore "sometimes" foods, or treats, and develop a greater understanding of why enjoying those foods in moderation is important to their health.

Physical fitness is also of the utmost importance for growing children, and it is suggested that they get at least 60 minutes per day of moderate to vigorous activity. At school and at home this can be difficult, since there is always so much to do. Still, knowing how important physical fitness is, we have to try! We have provided a variety of effective suggestions for exercises that can be done in the classroom. They can be completed in short increments on a daily basis. In addition to the obvious benefits of physical activity, the inclusion of purposeful physical activity at strategic times of the day can release tension and energize both students and teacher.

In recent years, the Common Core State Standards have been developed and are being implemented in many schools. These standards aim to prepare students for college and careers, with an emphasis on real-life applications. Coupled with the National Health Education Standards, they support a whole-child approach to education—one that ensures that each student is healthy, safe, engaged, supported, and challenged in his or her learning. The *Healthy Habits for Healthy Kids* series was developed to support this initiative.

How to Use This Book

Healthy Habits for Healthy Kids was developed to provide busy teachers and students with an easy-to-use curriculum to learn more about personal nutrition, health, and fitness. We want students to make healthy food choices and get exercise every day, knowing that healthier students make better learners.

Getting Started

- Share the Healthy Habits pledge (page 8) with students and discuss each line. Challenge students to learn the pledge and share it with family members. The goal is to inspire the whole family to focus on good nutrition and support healthy habits. Post the pledge in the classroom and review it from time to time as students gain more insights into their personal health.

- Introduce daily exercise and breathing activities in class. Use the suggestions on page 11 and the activity cards on pages 12 and 13 for movements that students can do for a minute or two during the day. Display a clock with a second hand or keep a timer handy for these sessions. Use the physical activities to start the day and/or to transition from one activity to another. Throw in an extra one on tough days, or use more than one when weather conditions inhibit outdoor activity. Short, physical exercise breaks are a positive way to settle students for their day's work. And don't forget those breathing exercises! They can be done at any time of day and can help refocus or calm students as needed.

Introduction *(cont.)*

How to Use This Book *(cont.)*

Getting Started *(cont.)*

- Gather and display reference materials for the classroom on topics of nutrition, fitness, and overall health. Resources might include library or trade books, magazines, posters, and kid-friendly materials printed from government websites (see page 5). If appropriate, save links to relevant websites in a dedicated folder on classroom computers.

- Encourage students to start collecting packaging and nutritional labels from food products. Explain that they will be learning to read them and using them for comparisons. Establish an area in the classroom where nutrition labels can be stored or displayed.

The Student Pages

Student pages present health-related information and activities. Discuss the information together as a class. Share information. Most activities require no more than writing implements and classroom research materials. Devote a certain amount of time each day or week to these activities. The more regular they are, the more important they will be for students.

You might consider interspersing the Healthy Foods activities with Healthy Habits activities to give students a balanced approach. As the teacher, you know how much information your students can absorb at a time. Be sensitive to the dietary needs and the family eating habits of your students.

There are three sections to this book. The first section, Healthy Foods, focuses on the five food groups as described in government materials such as ChooseMyPlate.gov. The goal is to educate students about healthy foods—what they look like, where they come from, what nutrients they provide, and how they can be incorporated into one's diet. A list of the foods in the food group is found at the beginning of each section. Have students think about the foods they eat regularly, the foods they have not heard of, and healthy foods to try. Provide resource materials for students to learn about foods that are new to them. Encourage students to think about ways they can make healthy food choices each day.

In the Healthy Habits section, students are introduced to concepts such as food safety, germ prevention, dental care, physical fitness, and other ways to stay safe and healthy.

Suggestions on pages 78–79 are for outdoor, gross-motor skills activities. These activities will allow students to explore a full range of motion: hopping, running, skipping, leaping, jumping, etc.

The final section of this book is devoted to journaling. The Food and Fitness Journal gives students opportunities to express their thoughts about the information presented in the activities and class discussions. The journal can be used for reflective writing, sorting or summarizing information, or to check for understanding.

Reproduce copies of the journal pages (88–92) for each student. Encourage students to add pages to the journal throughout the year as new food and fitness topics arise. Reproduce extra copies of the blank journal page provided on page 92 as needed.

The CD includes ready-to-print PDF files of the student activity pages and the Food and Fitness Journal, as well as correlations to the Common Core State Standards and the National Health Education Standards.

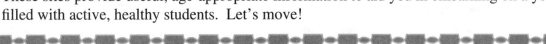

Internet Resources

These sites provide useful, age-appropriate information to aid you in embarking on a year filled with active, healthy students. Let's move!

Action for Healthy Kids
This site provides information for schools, students, and parents, as well as programs to promote active, healthy lifestyles for kids.
http://www.actionforhealthykids.org/

Fresh for Kids
This site offers resources for kids and teachers, including informative pages on specific fruits and vegetables.
http://www.freshforkids.com.au

Let's Move! America's Move to Raise a Healthier Generation of Kids
This program was developed by First Lady Michelle Obama to solve the epidemic of childhood obesity.
http://www.letsmove.gov/

National Farm to School Network
This site offers resources and information about farm-to-school programs in each state.
http://www.farmtoschool.org

Nourish Interactive
This site offers free printable activities based on the *ChooseMyPlate.gov* food groups.
http://www.nourishinteractive.com/nutrition-education

Tips for Healthy Eating—Ten Healthy Habits for Kids
This site includes a summary of ways families can incorporate healthy eating habits.
http://www.nestle.com/nhw/health-wellness-tips/healthy-habits-kids

USDA—United States Department of Agriculture
This site includes kid-friendly research, printable materials, and Nutrition Fact Cards.
http://www.choosemyplate.gov/print-materials-ordering.html

The Whole Child
This site focuses on ensuring that each child in each school and in each community is healthy, safe, engaged, supported, and challenged to meet the demands of the 21st century.
http://www.wholechildeducation.org/about

Whole Grains Council
The Whole Grains Council wants to support everyone who's helping spread the word about the health benefits of whole grains, and about easy ways to find and enjoy more whole grains.
http://wholegrainscouncil.org/resources/educational-materials

National Health Education Standards

The activities in *Healthy Habits for Healthy Kids (Kindergarten)* meet the following National Health Education Standards. For more information about these standards go to *www.cdc.gov/healthyyouth/sher/standards/index.htm*

Standard 1.2.1. Identify that healthy behaviors impact personal health.

Standard 1.2.2. Recognize that there are multiple dimensions of health.

Standard 1.2.3. Describe ways to prevent communicable diseases.

Standard 1.2.4. List ways to prevent common childhood injuries.

Standard 2.2.2. Identify what the school can do to support personal health practices and behaviors.

Standard 4.2.2. Demonstrate listening skills to enhance health.

Standard 5.2.1. Identify situations when a health-related decision is needed.

Standard 6.2.1. Identify a short-term personal health goal and take action toward achieving the goal.

Standard 7.2.1. Demonstrate healthy practices and behaviors to maintain or improve personal health.

Standard 7.2.2. Demonstrate behaviors to avoid or reduce health risks.

Standard 8.2.2. Encourage peers to make positive health choices.

Common Core State Standards Correlation

Each lesson or activity in *Healthy Habits for Healthy Kids (K)* meets one or more of the following Common Core State Standards © Copyright 2010. National Governors Association Center for Best Practices and Council of Chief State School Officers. All rights reserved. For more information about these standards, go to *http://www.corestandards.org/* or *http://www.teachercreated.com/standards/* for activities related to each standard.

Reading Informational Text

Key Ideas and Details

ELA.RI.K.1 With prompting and support, ask and answer questions about key details in a text.

ELA.RI.K.2 With prompting and support, identify the main topic and retell key details of a text.

Craft and Structure

ELA.RI.K.4 With prompting and support, ask and answer questions about unknown words in a text.

Writing

Text Types and Purposes

ELA.W.K.1 Use a combination of drawing, dictating, and writing to compose opinion pieces in which they tell a reader the topic or the name of the book they are writing about and state an opinion or preference about the topic or book (e.g., My favorite book is...).

ELA.W.K.2 Use a combination of drawing, dictating, and writing to compose informative/explanatory texts in which they name what they are writing about and supply some information about the topic.

Research to Build and Present Knowledge

ELA.W.K. 8 With guidance and support from adults, recall information from experiences or gather information from provided sources to answer a question.

Speaking & Listening

Comprehension and Collaboration

ELA.SL.K.1 Participate in collaborative conversations with diverse partners about kindergarten topics and texts with peers and adults in small and larger groups.

ELA.SL.K.2 Confirm understanding of a text read aloud or information presented orally or through other media by asking and answering questions about key details and requesting clarification if something is not understood.

Presentation of Knowledge and Ideas

ELA.SL.K.5 Add drawings or other visual displays to descriptions as desired to provide additional detail.

Language

Conventions of Standard English

ELA.L.K.1 Demonstrate command of the conventions of standard English grammar and usage when writing or speaking.

ELA.L.K.2 Demonstrate command of the conventions of standard English capitalization, punctuation, and spelling when writing.

Vocabulary Acquisition and Use

ELA.L.K.4 Determine or clarify the meaning of unknown and multiple-meaning words and phrases based on kindergarten reading and content.

ELA.L.K.5a Sort common objects into categories (e.g., shapes, foods) to gain a sense of the concepts the categories represent.

ELA.L.K.6 Use words and phrases acquired through conversations, reading and being read to, and responding to texts.

Take the Pledge

Practice the "Healthy Habits Pledge." Then, take it home and read or recite it to a family member. Sign your name at the bottom of the page and bring it back to school.

Healthy Habits Pledge

I pledge to stay healthy and clean

through exercise and good hygiene.

I will eat balanced meals every day

to have more energy to learn and to play.

Every night I will get a good rest

to be more ready to do my best.

If I work hard to be healthy and strong,

I'll be happier my whole life long.

I, _____,

have learned the Healthy Habits Pledge.

Introducing the 5 Food Groups

This book refers to the five food groups as listed on ChooseMyPlate.gov. (*www.choosemyplate.gov.*) The table below lists foods in their true columns. See the notes below for exceptions for purposes of discussion with students.

Fruits

apples	grapes	mangoes	plums
apple juice	grape juice	nectarines	raisins
apricots	grapefruit	oranges	raspberries
bananas	grapefruit juice	orange juice	strawberries
blackberries	honeydew	papayas	tangerines
blueberries	kiwi fruit	peaches	watermelons
cantaloupe	lemons	pears	
cherries	limes	pineapples	

Vegetables

artichoke	carrots	lentils	spinach
asparagus	cauliflower	lima beans	split peas
bean sprouts	celery	mushrooms	sweet potatoes
beets	corn	navy beans	taro
black beans	eggplant	onions	turnips
black-eyed peas	garbanzo beans	peas	water chestnuts
bok choy	iceberg lettuce	pinto beans	wax beans
broccoli	kale	potatoes	white beans
Brussels sprouts	kidney beans	romaine lettuce	
cabbage	leaf lettuce	soybeans	

Culinary or Fruit Vegetables

avocados	green beans	pumpkins	squash
cucumbers	green peppers	red peppers	tomatoes

Important Distinctions

We define *fruit* as the sweet, fleshy part of a plant. Any part of a plant we eat that is *not* the fruit, may be considered a vegetable. By this definition, vegetables can include *leaves, stems, roots, flowers, bulbs,* and *seeds*.

Culinary or Fruit Vegetables—We know that *fruit* refers to the flowering part of a plant in which seeds develop. By this definition, many foods we consider vegetables are actually fruits. Often, these foods are prepared or eaten as vegetables, so we call them "culinary vegetables" or "fruit vegetables."

Introducing the 5 Food Groups (cont.)

Grains

Whole Grains		Refined Grain Foods
amaranth	rolls	cereals
barley	rye	corn tortillas
brown rice	sorghum	cornbread
buckwheat	triticale	couscous
bulger (cracked wheat)	whole grain cereal	crackers
cornmeal	whole wheat	flour tortillas
millet	whole wheat bread	grits
muesli	whole wheat crackers	noodles
oatmeal	whole wheat pasta	pasta
popcorn	whole wheat tortillas	pitas
quinoa	wild rice	white bread
rolled oats		white rice

Dairy

cheddar cheese	greek yogurt	parmesan cheese	swiss cheese
cottage cheese	milk	pudding	yogurt
frozen yogurt	mozzarella cheese	ricotta cheese	

Protein

almonds	duck	lima beans	sesame seeds
beef	eggs	navy beans	soybeans
bison	fish	nuts	split peas
black beans	goose	peanuts	sunflower seeds
black-eyed peas	ham	pinto beans	turkey
cashews	hazelnuts	pork	veal
chicken	kidney beans	pumpkin seeds	venison
chickpeas	lamb	rabbit	walnuts

* also ground beef, chicken, lamb, pork, or turkey

Exercise of the Day

Here are some tips to get your daily indoor exercise program started.

1. Each day, ask a student to choose an exercise card for the class to perform: Use the cards on pages 12–13.

2. Demonstrate the exercises on each card as needed. Point out the parts of the body being used. When the movement involves stretching, suggest slow and steady movements.

3. Ask questions that pertain to the movements.

   • How long can you make your arms or legs when you reach?

   • How fast can you run in place?

   • Can you run in slow motion?

   • When you pretend to climb a tree, do your hands and feet move together or do they alternate?

4. Set a timer or watch the clock, and do each day's activity for one minute.

5. Add the chosen card to your class calendar each morning after the students have completed the action.

6. Repeat the same action throughout the day to signal transitions or simply to give students an opportunity to stretch and refocus their energies.

"Exercise of the Day" Cards

Touch toes. Reach up.

Pretend to hula hoop.

Hop on one foot.

Run in place.

Do jumping jacks.

Make large arm circles.

March in place.

Pretend to climb stairs.

Do lunges or squats.

Do slow shoulder scrunches.

Do slow neck rolls.

Dance.

"Exercise of the Day" Cards *(cont.)*

Do desk pushups.

Do chair squats.

Pretend to jump rope.

Sit and pretend to pedal.

Tiptoe stretch.

Do leg raises.

Twist.

Sway like tall grass in the wind.

Lean left, then right.

Lean forward, then back.

Wiggle hips.

Hop in place on 2 feet.

Name

Healthy Foods

The Food We Eat

We eat many different kinds of foods. Some foods come from plants.
Some foods come from animals. Look at the picture below.

    1. Color the plants that give us food.

    2. Color the animals we get food from.

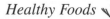

How Do We Get Our Food?

Trucks bring food to stores. We shop for food. Draw food in the cart.

What food is in your cart? _____

_____

_____

1. Does your family grow food? **YES**   **NO**

2. Does your family buy food at a farmers' market? **YES**   **NO**

3. Does your family shop at the grocery store? **YES**   **NO**

Fruits Checklist 1

Many fruits come from trees. They are different shapes and sizes. Put an **X** next to each fruit you have tried. Circle the ones you would like to try.

Citrus Fruits with Seeds	Fruits with Stones
☐ grapefruit	☐ apricot
☐ lemon	☐ cherry
☐ lime	☐ nectarine
☐ orange	☐ peach
☐ tangerine	☐ plum

More Fruits with Seeds	
☐ apple	☐ pear

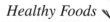

Fruits Checklist 2

Some fruits grow on trees. Others grow on plants, vines, or "runners" on the ground. They are different shapes and sizes. Put an **X** next to each fruit you have tried. Circle the ones you would like to try.

Berries	Tropical Fruits
☐ blueberries	☐ banana
☐ grapes	☐ mango
☐ kiwi fruit	☐ papaya
☐ raspberries	☐ pineapple
☐ strawberries	

Melons

☐ cantaloupe   ☐ honeydew   ☐ watermelon

Healthy Foods

Seeds on the Outside!

Most fruits have seeds on the inside. One fruit has its seeds on the outside.

Directions: Connect the dots to discover a fruit that has seeds on the outside!

1. What color is this fruit? _____

2. Circle the name of this fruit.

cherry   banana   strawberry

Fruits Grow on Trees

Some fruits grow on trees. We can pick the fruit off the tree and eat it.

Directions: Color the pictures. Trace the name of each fruit.

Name two other fruits that grow on trees.

_____   _____

Same Fruit, Different Colors

Pears can be different colors. Pears can be different shapes.

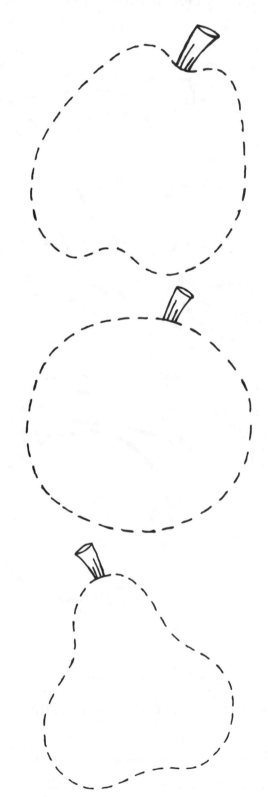

1. This is an **Anjou pear.**
   Trace it and color it red.

2. This is an **Asian pear**.
   Trace it and color it yellow.

3. This is a **Bartlett pear**.
   Trace it and color it green.

4. Circle the pears you have tasted.

Fruits Grow on Vines and Bushes

Some fruits grow on vines. A vine has a long stem. It climbs on the ground or can go up a fence. Other fruits, called berries, grow on bushes.
Directions: Color the pictures and fill in the blanks.

1. Grapes grow on vines. Grapes are _____, purple, or green.

2. Blueberries grow on bushes.

   They are _____.

3. Raspberries grow on bushes.

   They are _____.

Fruits Are Good for Us

Directions: Draw a line to match each fruit to its name. Color the pictures.

1.

banana

2.

peach

3.

plum

4.

pineapple

5.

watermelon

Vegetables Checklist 1

We eat different parts of different vegetables. For some, we eat the *leaves* and for others the *roots* or *flowers*. How many of these vegetables have you tasted? Put an **X** by each one. Circle the ones you would like to try.

Leaf Vegetables

☐ cabbage

☐ chard

☐ kale

☐ lettuce

☐ spinach

Root Vegetables

☐ beets

☐ carrots

☐ daikon

☐ radishes

☐ turnips

Flower and Bud Vegetables

☐ artichoke

☐ asparagus

☐ broccoli

☐ cauliflower

Vegetables Checklist 2

Some vegetables grow in pods. Others have seeds like fruits but we cook them like vegetables. How many of these vegetables have you tasted? Put an **X** by each one. Circle the ones you would like to try.

Vegetables in Pods

☐ green beans

☐ runner beans

☐ kidney beans

☐ snow peas

☐ lima beans

☐ sugar snap peas

☐ peas

☐ wax beans

☐ pinto beans

Culinary or Fruit Vegetables

☐ cucumbers

☐ tomato

☐ eggplant

☐ zucchini

☐ pumpkin

24

Squash—Vegetable or Fruit?

Squash have seeds on the inside. They are a fruit, but people call them vegetables because they are often cooked before they are eaten.

1. Look at the pictures. Circle the names of each squash.

2. Count the seeds and write the number in the box.

How many seeds?

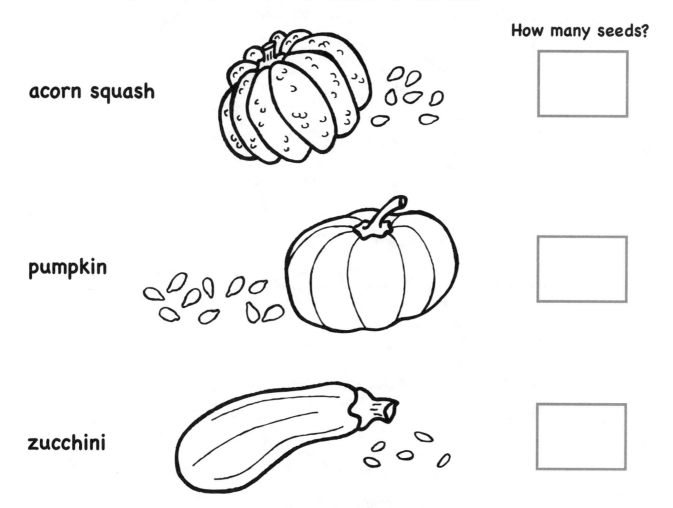

acorn squash

pumpkin

zucchini

3. Squash can be eaten many ways. Circle the ways you have tried it.

bread   pie   soup   with butter

Traffic Light Peppers

Peppers have seeds inside. They are fruits that we eat like vegetables. They can be cooked. They can be different colors and shapes.

Directions: Does this look like a traffic light? Color the peppers red, yellow, and green.

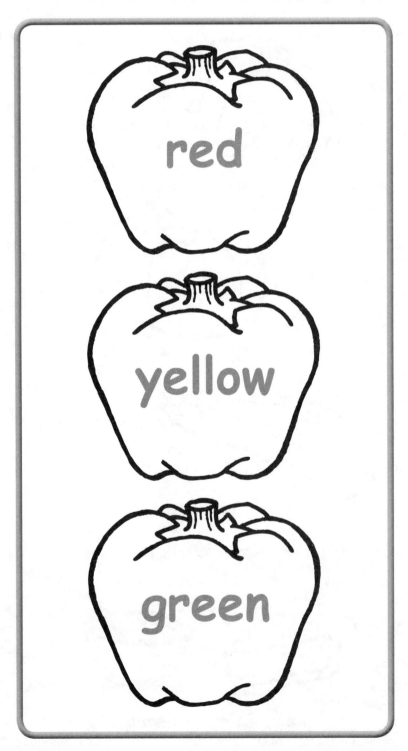

Many Kinds of Tomatoes

Tomatoes grow on vines. They can be different sizes and shapes. We can eat them right off the vine or we can cook them.

1. Color the tomatoes.

2. Count them and write the totals in the boxes.

cherry tomatoes

grape tomatoes

Roma tomatoes

beefsteak tomato

3. Circle the ways you enjoy eating tomatoes.

spaghetti sauce

slices

whole tomatoes

salsa

Leaf Vegetables

We eat the leaves of some vegetable plants. They grow in gardens and on farms. They are very good for us.

1. Color the four leafy green vegtables.

| spinach | lettuce | kale | cabbage |

2. Circle the vegetable in each row that is not a leafy green vegetable.

Row 1

spinach   carrots   lettuce

Row 2

kale   cabbage   green beans

Eating Orange Roots!

Carrots are vegetables that grow in the ground. The part we eat is the root!

1. How many carrots do you see?

2. How do you like to eat carrots? Circle your choices.

| with dip | cooked | carrot cake | raw |

Hidden Vegetables

Directions: Use the color code to find the hidden vegetables.

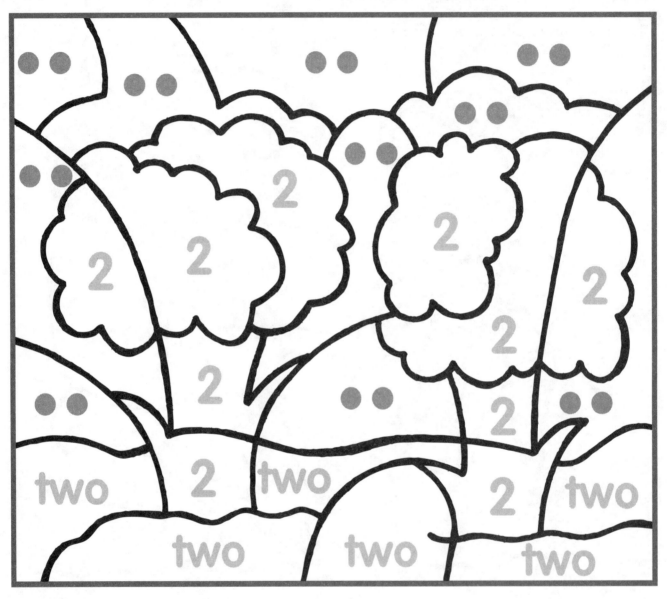

two = brown   2 = green   •• = blue

How many broccoli stalks do you see? _____ Broccoli is an important vegetable to eat. We get vitamins and fiber from broccoli.

A Purple Vegetable

Do you know what it is? This vegetable has the word *egg* as part of its name, but it is not an egg!

1. Connect the dots to discover this vegetable.

2. Color the vegetable purple. Color the leaves of this vegetable green.

3. Trace the name of this vegetable.

eggplant

Name

Garden Maze

Can you get to the healthy salad in the garden maze? Start at the garden gate.

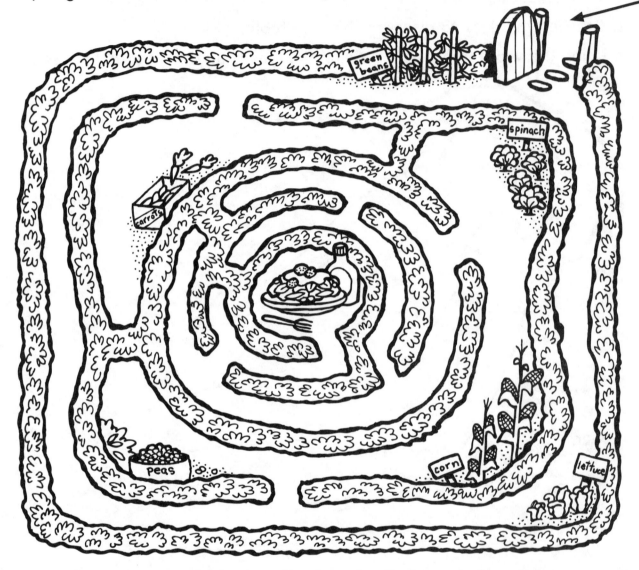

Color the garden vegetables you like to eat. Circle your favorite.

carrots	lettuce	green beans
spinach	corn	peas

32   © Teacher Created Resources, Inc.

Grains Checklist

Oats, wheat, corn, barley, and rice are important grains. We eat them or use them to make flour to make breads, pasta, crackers, or tortillas. Circle the ones you have eaten. Draw a box around a grain food you would like to try.

Wheat

whole wheat bread   pita   cereal   whole wheat crackers   whole wheat pasta   whole wheat tortilla

Oats

oatmeal   oat snack bar   oat bread   oat scones

Corn

corn cereal   corn tortilla   cornbread   popcorn   cornmeal

Barley and Rice

soup   brown rice   wild rice   white rice

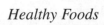

The Little Red Hen

Remember the story of the Little Red Hen? She grew wheat to make wheat flour. Then she made healthy bread. Her friends did not help her. It was a lot of work all by herself! Cut out the pictures and make a book to color.

The
Little
Red Hen

Name: _____

She planted seeds. (1)

She watered the wheat. (2)

She cut the wheat. (3)

The Little Red Hen *(cont.)*

Teacher Note: Make copies of pages 34 and 35. Students will use the guidelines on page 34 to cut the pictures out and then assemble. Read and discuss the story.

She ground the wheat. ④

She mixed the ingredients. ⑤

She baked the bread. ⑥

She made wheat bread! ⑦

Whole Grains—Wheat

Wheat is grown on farms. Huge machines cut it and put it in trucks.

Circle your favorite food made with wheat. Color the foods.

| pasta | tortillas | wheat bread | cereal |

Whole Grains—Oats

Oats are a whole grain food. Whole grain foods help us grow healthy and strong.

1. Oats grow in fields. Color the oats growing in the field green.

2. Color the oats ready to be harvested yellow or light brown.

3. Circle the foods made with oats that you like to eat. Put a box around one you might want try.

oatmeal   **oat bread**   **oat bar**   **oat cereal**

Whole Grains—Corn

Many people eat corn. Corn is a whole grain. It grows on stalks in fields.

1. Color the ear of corn below.

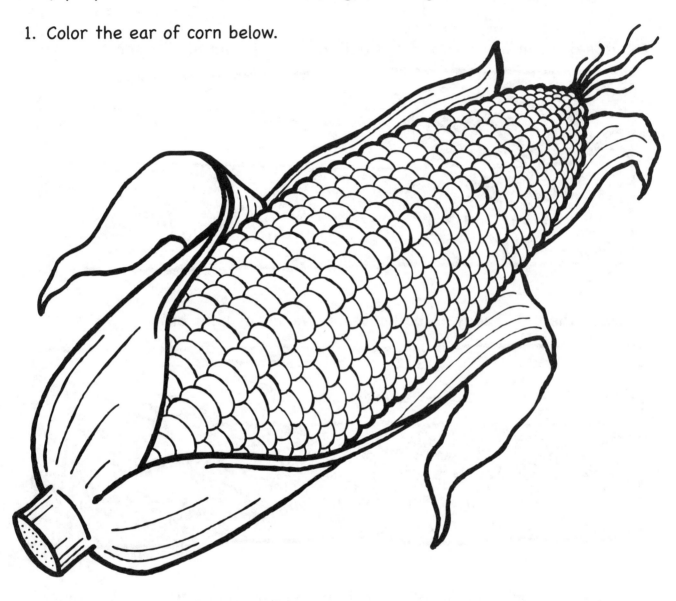

2. Circle your favorite way to eat corn. Color the foods.

corn on the cob   **corn**   **cornbread**   **corn taco**

Name

Healthy Foods

Whole Grains—Barley

Barley is a whole grain. You can add it to soup, or it can be a side dish. Here is a traditional folk song about barley and how it grows. Act it out as you sing!

Oats, Peas, Beans, and Barley Grow

Chorus
Oats, peas, beans, and barley grow,
Oats, peas, beans, and barley grow,
Do you, or I, or anyone know
How oats, peas, beans, and barley grow?

First, the farmer sows the seed,
Stands erect and takes his ease,
Stamps his feet and claps his hands,
And turns around to view the lands.
(Repeat *Chorus*)

Next, the farmer waters the seeds,
Stands erect and takes his ease,
Stamps his feet and claps his hands,
And turns around to view the lands.
(Repeat *Chorus*)

Next, the farmer hoes the weeds.
Stands erect and takes his ease,
Stamps his feet and claps his hands,
And turns around to view the lands.
(Repeat *Chorus*)

Last, the farmer harvests his seeds,
Stands erect and takes his ease,
Stamps his feet and claps his hands,
And turns around to view the lands.
(Repeat *Chorus*)

Whole Grains—Brown Rice

Brown rice is good for us. It is a healthy whole grain food.

Directions: Color the rice light brown. Choose your favorite colors to color the bowl.

Dairy Checklist

Dairy foods give us calcium to help us grow strong bones and teeth.

1. Put an **X** in the box near each dairy food you have tasted.
2. Circle the dairy foods you would like to try.

Dairy

☐ milk   ☐ yogurt   ☐ Greek yogurt

Cheeses

☐ string cheese   ☐   ☐ cottage cheese

parmesan

☐ cheddar   ☐ mozzarella   ☐ ricotta   ☐ swiss cheese

Dairy Treats

Some dairy products are treats. They are "sometimes" foods. They taste good, but it is best not to eat them every day.

☐ pudding   ☐ frozen yogurt   ☐ ice cream

Where Does Milk Come From?

Milk comes from cows. How do we get milk? Trace the path and see!

1. **Farmers milk the cows.**

2. The milk goes in containers.

3. **The containers go to the stores.**

4. **We buy milk at the store.**

Dairy Foods

Dairy foods are made from milk. These foods have calcium to help us build strong bones and teeth. It is best to choose dairy foods that are low in fat.

Directions: Cross out the food in each row that is not a dairy food.

Row 1

milk   cheese   broccoli

Row 2

yogurt   apple   milk

Row 3

corn on the cob   pudding   cheddar cheese

Find the Dairy Food

Directions: Complete the dot-to-dot to find a healthy dairy food.

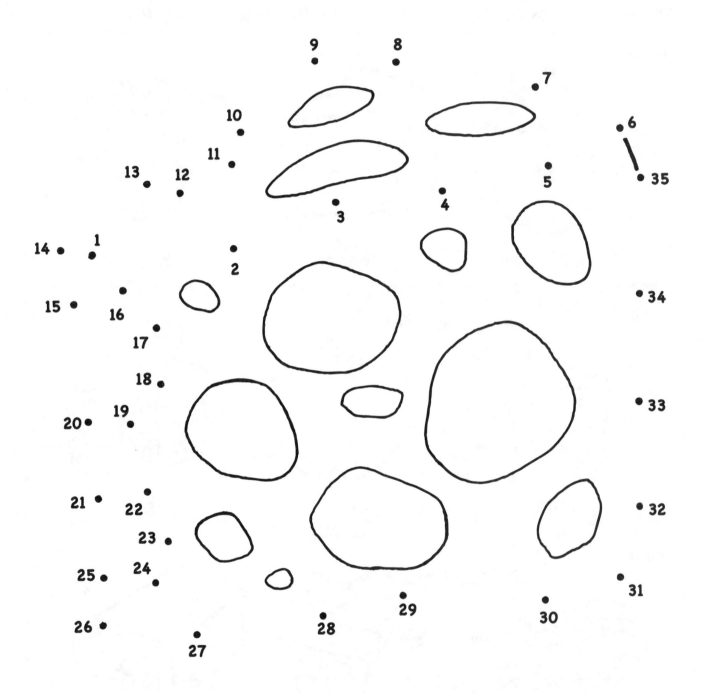

What did you find? _____

My Dairy Foods

Dairy foods are good for us! They help us grow strong bones and teeth.

Directions: Draw a picture of yourself eating the healthy dairy food you like best. Name the dairy food.

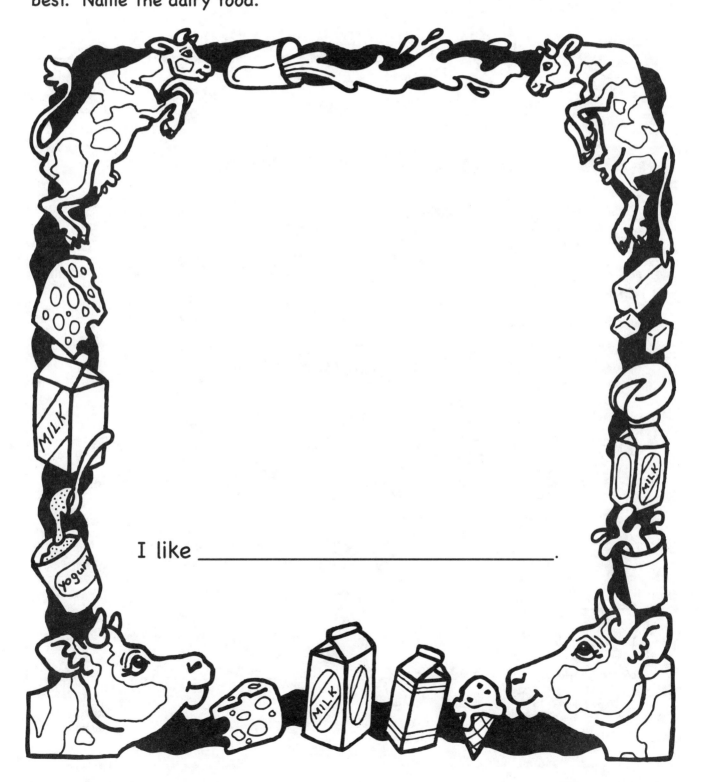

I like _____.

Protein Checklist

Directions: Color each protein food you have tasted. Circle foods you would like to try.

Poultry and Eggs

goose

turkey

eggs

chicken

duck

Nuts, Seeds, and Legumes

pumpkin seeds

almonds

sunflower seeds

hazelnuts

sesame seeds

walnuts

cashews

peanuts

Beans and Peas

lima beans

black beans

pinto beans

black-eyed peas

split peas

kidney beans

navy beans

chickpeas

Meats

beef
(cow)

rabbit

bison

lamb

ham
(pig)

venison
(deer)

Name _____

Healthy Foods

Protein

Protein helps keep our muscles strong so that we can move. Protein gives us energy.

Directions: Write the name of each protein food under its picture. Use the Word Bank to help you.

Word Bank					
beans	eggs	fish	meat	nuts	seeds

Protein Makes Us Strong

We can think of protein as building blocks. Protein makes our muscles strong.
Protein keeps our heart and lungs healthy.

Directions: Color the pictures of all the protein foods.

Nuts Are Protein, Too!

Nuts grow on trees. Nuts are a healthy protein food. They give us energy.

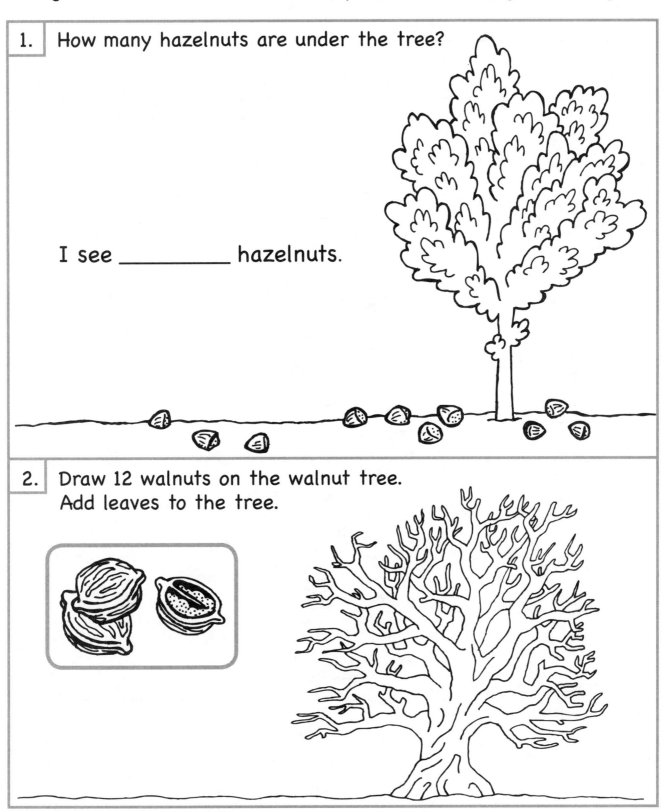

1. How many hazelnuts are under the tree?

   I see _____ hazelnuts.

2. Draw 12 walnuts on the walnut tree.
   Add leaves to the tree.

Name

Foods of Every Color

Healthy foods come in many colors. What is your favorite food color?

_____

Color Word Bank							
red	brown	blue	orange	green	white	purple	yellow

Directions: Use the Color Word Bank to find a color for each healthy food.

1. strawberries    _____

2. blueberries    _____

3. plum    _____

4. wheat bread    _____

5. corn 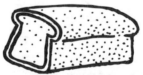   _____

6. milk    _____

7. lettuce    _____

8. orange    _____

Food Groups

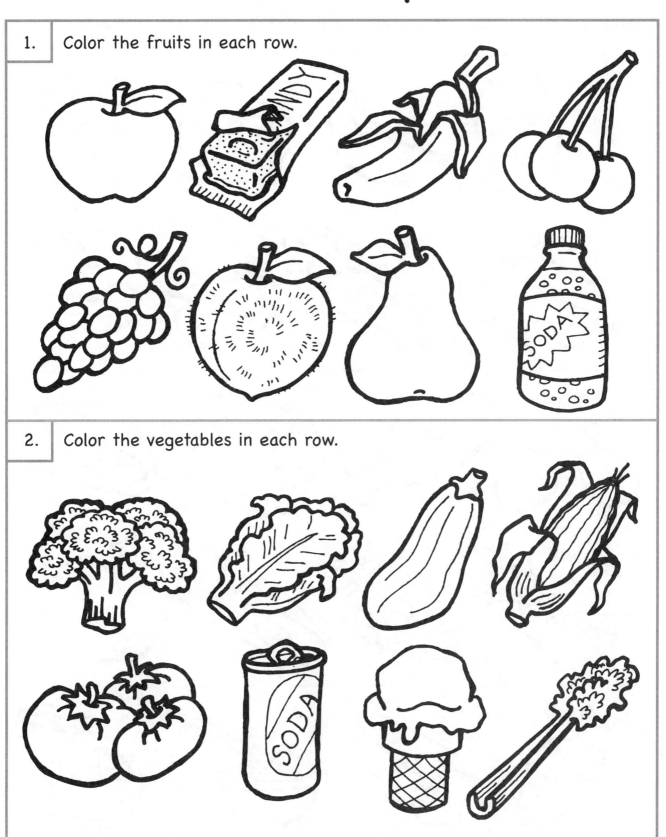

1. Color the fruits in each row.

2. Color the vegetables in each row.

More Food Groups

Directions: Circle the food in each row that does not belong in the food group.

1. Dairy
2. Vegetables
3. Protein
4. Fruits
5. Whole Grains

Which Group?

Directions: Draw a line from each food to its food group.

Eat Healthy Foods

Directions: Circle the three foods shown in the picture. Write the name of each one on the lines in the box. Color the picture.

I eat healthy foods.

p _ _ _ s   a _ _ _ _ s

c _ _ _ _ _ s

Name

My Favorites

Directions: Draw your favorite healthy food and your favorite treat.

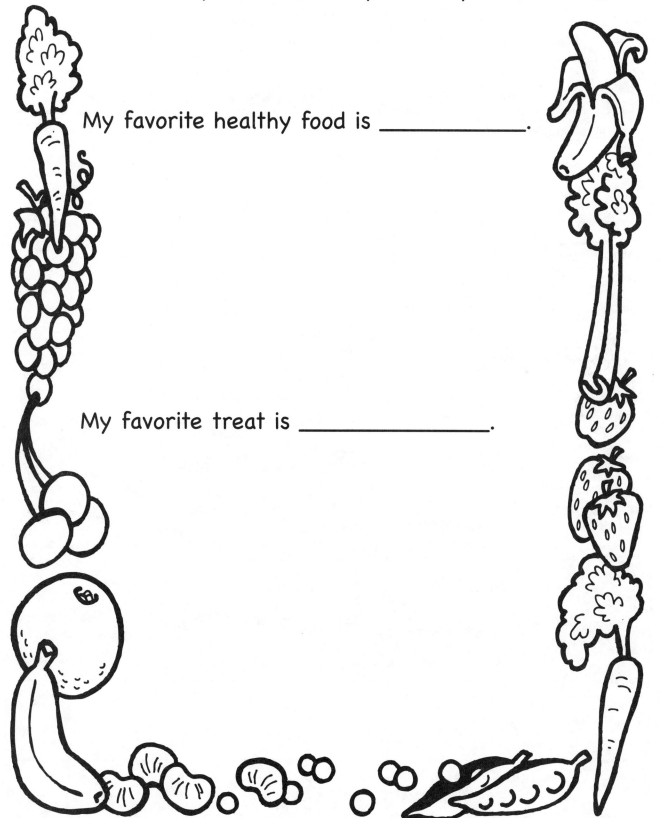

My favorite healthy food is _____.

My favorite treat is _____.

Healthy Foods Chart

Sam is a healthy eater. He tries to eat foods from all the food groups.
  1. Count how many foods he ate from each group.
  2. Write the totals under the chart.

Sam's Healthy Foods

Fruits	Vegetables	Grains	Protein	Dairy

Sam's Totals

Foods to Know

Have you had these healthy foods before? Say their names and count the syllables. Now let's name the food group for each one. Check the box if you have had this healthy food before.

1. asparagus

2. barley

3. broccoli

4. soybeans (edamame)

5. kiwi fruit

6. mango

7. oatmeal

8. yogurt

Find the Healthy Foods

Ben went to a fair with his family. He wanted something healthy to eat.

1. Color the healthy food choices in the picture.

2. Circle a treat Ben might choose to eat.

Health Tip: Some foods have more sugar or fat. We call these foods treats or *sometimes* foods. Save these foods for special days.

Make Healthy Choices

Try eating healthy foods every day. They will help you grow and be strong.

1. Color these healthy food choices. Circle your two favorites.

2. Some foods are not for every day. These treats or "sometimes" foods are not as good for our bodies. Color your two favorite treats.

Keep Food Safe

Directions: Talk about these three ways to keep food safe. Color each picture.

Wash your hands before eating.

Keep fresh foods in the refrigerator.

Use clean plates and utensils.

Stay Healthy

Here are some things we do to stay healthy. Do them every day.

Directions: Draw a line from each healthy idea to its picture.

1.) Eat a good breakfast.

2.) Brush your teeth.

3.) Get exercise.

4.) Drink water.

5.) Eat healthy snacks.

6.) Get plenty of sleep.

Sleep and Rest

Our bodies need to rest. If we don't get enough rest or sleep we get cranky and don't think as clearly. Rest helps us do better in school and sports.

1. Put a box around pictures of children who are resting.

2. Circle the pictures of children playing.

Wash Your Hands

1. Cut out each picture that shows when you should wash your hands.
2. Glue the pictures in the boxes.

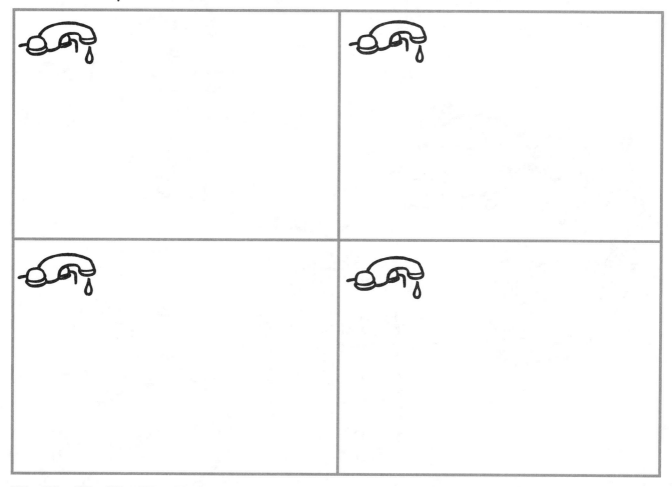

What Do You Use?

Directions: Circle the things that you use to wash your hands.   Color them.

If You Are Sick

1. Circle two pictures in each row that show things you should do when you are sick.
2. Cross out the picture in each row that shows a way that germs spread.

Row 1	Rest and drink water.

Row 2	Be careful when you cough.

Row 3	Try not to spread germs.

Teeth Need Care

It is important to take care of our teeth. Brush, floss, and get checkups.

Directions: Color the ways you take care of your teeth.

1. Brush your teeth.

2. Floss your teeth.

3. Go to the dentist.

4. Make healthy food choices.

Be Safe

Directions: Cross out the pictures in each row of things that are not safe to do.

Row 1

Cross at a crosswalk.

Row 2

Follow safety rules on the playground.

Follow the directions in each box below to make each child safer.

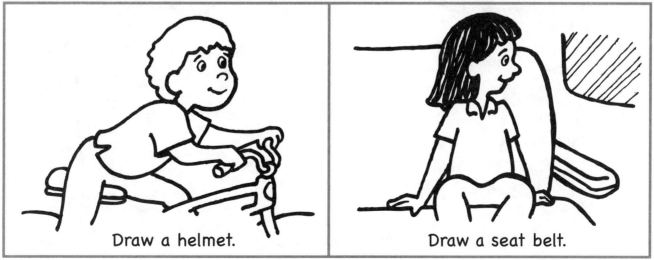

Draw a helmet.

Draw a seat belt.

Stretch and Move

Stretching helps us breathe. It helps us play sports better. It helps us move. Try this rhyme and stretch!

Head, Shoulders, Knees and Toes

Head, shoulders, knees and toes,
knees and toes,

Head, shoulders, knees and toes,
knees and toes,

And eyes and ears and mouth and nose,

Head, shoulders, knees and toes,
knees and toes!

1. Look at the pictures below. Watch your teacher and try these stretches.
2. Can you stretch to the right and then stretch to the left?

3. Try other chants or rhymes when you stretch.

Name

Moving in Place

Did you know you could stay in one place and exercise? You can!

Directions: Stand and try these moves. Color your favorite one.

1. Hop in place 10 times.
   Can you do 20 hops?

2. March in place. Sing a song.

3. Run in place for one minute.

4. Do 10 jumping jacks.

Moving Every Day

Each day we move in different ways. Look at the pictures. What is each child doing? Copy the movements.

Directions: Use the Word Box to help you label each picture below.

| Word Bank | bend | climb | squat | stretch |

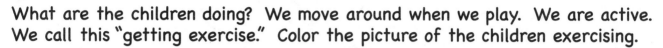

Healthy Actions

What are the children doing? We move around when we play. We are active.
We call this "getting exercise." Color the picture of the children exercising.

I exercise my body by _____

_____ .

Playground Fun

1. The playground is a place to exercise. Draw a line from the exercise word to the activity.

Climb

Slide

Swing

2. Color the things you can use to get exercise.

Make Your Own Music

We listen to music. Sometimes we dance to music. We can make our own music. You can make music even if you do not have instruments. Try making music by following the directions below.

1. Tap a rhythm on the desk.
   Do it fast! Do it slow!

2. Stomp your feet.
   Stomp hard!
   Stomp gently!

3. Clap your hands.
   Clap up high!
   Clap down low!

4. Combine all three actions.
   Tap three times.
   Stomp three times.
   Clap three times.

   Repeat. Add on.

Variation: Stand up. Tap the rhythm on your thighs, stomp your feet, and clap your hands above your head. Repeat.

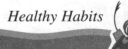

Move to Music

Dance

Dancing is one way we move to music. It helps us stay healthy.

1. Play some music and dance to it.

2. Use your arms and legs.

3. Dance faster or slower as the music changes.

Variations: Play Freeze Dance or Musical Chairs.

Marching Parade

Have you ever watched people in a parade? They walk or march to music.

1. Play some marching music.

2. Line up and follow a leader.

3. Pretend to wave a flag or a baton or play musical instruments.

4. March in place or around the room.

Move Like an Animal

Animals move in many different ways. Some crawl, some run, and some climb. Others fly or swing.

Directions: Find an open area and move like these animals.

Check the box after each one you try.

☐ 1. Climb like a monkey, hand over hand.

☐ 2. Pace like a mountain lion.
Get on all fours.

☐ 3. Jump like a kangaroo.
How high can you jump? How far?

☐ 4. Be a large bird. Flap and glide.

☐ 5. Be a small bird and flutter your arms.

☐ 6. Waddle like a penguin.

More Animal Moves

Animals move in many different ways. Can you move like these animals?

Directions: Check the box after each one you try.

☐ Move like a big bear.

☐ Wiggle like an octopus.

☐ Hop like a frog.

☐ Balance on one leg like a flamingo.

☐ Walk like a giraffe.

☐ Swim like a fish.

Circus Fun

Make a "tightrope" on the floor. Use a long piece of string or tape. Ask students to imagine that they are walking on a real tightrope. Here are some tips for them:

1. Hold your hands out to balance.

2. Look ahead, not down.

3. Place one foot right in front of the other.

4. Walk from one end to the other.

More Tight Rope Fun

1. Walk backward on the tightrope.

2. Hop on one foot on the tightrope.

3. Hop from side to side over the tightrope. Try not to step on it.

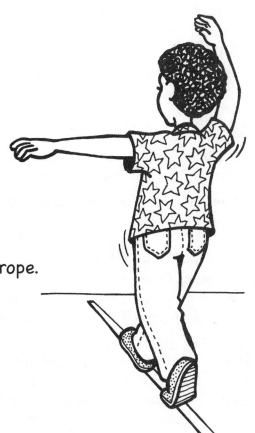

Variation: Think of other circus tricks or tumbling you could do in the classroom.

Ideas for Outdoors

Start with these transitions to go in and out of the classroom. Explain that each day students will walk out one way and come back into the classroom doing the opposite movement. Here are a few suggestions to get started:

- Walk out on heels, walk in on toes.
- Walk out quickly, walk in slowly.
- Walk out going forward, walk backward or sideways to return to the classroom.
- Slouch walking out, stand tall walking back in.
- Walk outside with arms in front, walk inside with arms behind back.
- Walk out in a straight line, walk in in a curvy line.

Foot Races

Try races doing different "traveling" movements. Use markers like traffic cones or coffee cans to signal starting and stopping points. Start with short distances and extend them as students' skills and stamina increase. Alternate laps of running, skipping, hopping on one foot or two feet, sliding sideways, or galloping.

Line Games

Play whole-group line games such as "Mother May I?," "Simon Says," or "Red Light, Green Light."

Circle Games

Involve the whole-group in circles games such as "Farmer in the Dell," "Ring Around the Rosie," or "Duck, Duck, Goose."

Teacher Note: If possible, when playing these games, consider two groups of 10 or more instead of one whole-class group. This will allow for more turns!

Combined Locomotor Skills

Use chalk to make locomotor movement signs and a large circle on the pavement. Try these words for starters: jump, run, hop, and slide.

Have groups of students take turns doing the different actions as they progress around the outside of the circle (so as not to step on the words). The circle can be enlarged as students become more comfortable with the different movements.

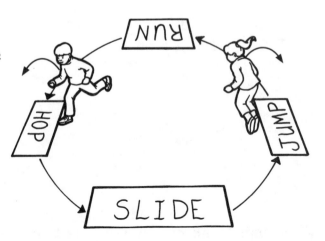

Ideas for Outdoors *(cont.)*

Scarf Tosses

Use old scarves or 12" squares of fabric. Have students follow a series of directions using the scarves. To start, allow students ample time to practice tossing the scarves up and catching them before they hit the ground. Encourage students to toss the scarves up as high as they can and then let them float down.

Then, try the following ideas:

- Toss the scarf with left hand and catch with right hand.
  Then switch to tossing with the right and catching with the left.
- Toss the scarf, turn around once, and try to catch the scarf before it floats to the ground.
- Toss and catch the scarf with a partner.

Beach Ball Toss

Tossing, bouncing, and catching a ball are all fun activities that can be done outside or seated in the classroom.

Take a few minutes to label the ball with words, letters, or numbers.

Have students arrange themselves in a circle.

Explain to students that they will toss the ball back and forth until they hear a signal.

The student who has the ball at the signal will read the word, letter, or number written on the ball closest to his or her right thumb.

Consider creating balls for students to practice one of the following skills:

- Letter identification
- Sight words
- Word recognition
- Rhyming with the word on the ball
- Addition facts
- Subtraction facts

Ball Rolling

Rolling a ball involves a number of skills including eye-hand coordination. To start, have students sit in a circle with legs crossed and knees touching. Have each student practice rolling and catching the ball across the circle.

Food and Fitness JOURNAL

This journal belongs to:

Being Healthy

Being healthy is important. What does it mean to be healthy?

When you are healthy, you can _____.

Here is what I look like when I _____.

To be healthy, you need to:

1. _____

_____

2. _____

_____

My Favorite Fruit

My favorite fruit is _____.

It grows _____.

It is _____.

Here is what it looks like when my favorite fruit is growing.

My Favorite Vegetable

My favorite vegetable is _____.

It grows _____.

It is _____.

Here is what it looks like when my favorite vegetable is growing.

My Favorite Protein Food

My favorite protein food is _____.

It comes from _____.

It is _____.

Here is what it looks like when my favorite protein food is growing.

My Favorite Dairy Food

My favorite dairy food is _____.

It comes from _____.

It is _____.

Here is where my favorite dairy food comes from.

My Favorite Grain Food

My favorite grain food is _____.

It grows _____.

It is _____.

Here is how my favorite grain food grows.

My Most Important Foods

I have learned about the five food groups. Here is a drawing of a food I eat from each group. I know it is a healthy food for me.

Fruit: _____

It is good for me because

_____

Vegetable: _____

It is good for me because

_____

Protein: _____

It is good for me because

_____

Dairy product: _____

It is good for me because

_____

Grain product: _____

It is good for me because

_____

If I was a farmer, I would like to grow _____

_____

My Healthy Meal

This is a healthy meal. I have added foods from every food group.

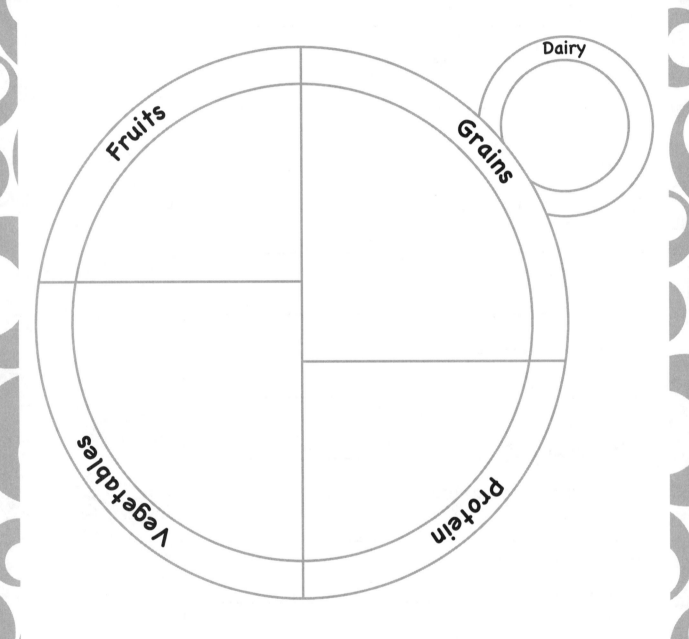

88 © Teacher Created Resources, Inc.

Making Good Choices

We are learning about healthy foods and "sometimes" foods. It is important to eat healthy foods at every meal. Sometimes foods are special treats for special times.

Sometimes Foods

"Sometimes" foods
are a special treat.
Some are salty
and some are sweet.

They are yummy
and can make you smile.
But only eat them
once in a while!

Eat healthy foods
to learn and grow.
And you'll be happy,
don't you know!

My favorite treats are: _____

_____

_____

Fighting Germs

Germs can make you sick. There are ways to stay healthy and keep germs away. Here are some things you can do.

1. _____

   _____

2. _____

   _____

Being Active

It is important to get exercise every day.

At school, I get exercise by _____

_____

At home, I get exercise by _____

_____

Journal Entry

_____

_____

_____

_____

_____

_____

_____

_____

_____

_____

Answer Key

page 14 (The Food We Eat)
1. *plants:* apples, corn
2. *animals:* pig, cow, hen

page 15 (How Do We Get Our Food?)
Answers will vary.

page 16 (Fruits Checklist 1)
Answers will vary.

page 17 (Fruit Checklist 2)
Answers will vary.

page 18 (Seeds on the Outside!)
Check student work on the dot-to-dot.
1. red
2. strawberry

page 19 (Fruits Grow on Trees)
Possible answers:
cherry, peach, plum, apricot, nectarine

page 20 (Same Fruit, Different Colors)
Check coloring for accuracy and understanding.

page 21 (Fruits Grow on Vines and Bushes)
1. red
2. blue
3. red

page 22 (Fruits Are Good for Us)
1. peach
2. plum
3. watermelon
4. banana
5. pineapple

page 23 (Vegetables Checklist 1)
Answers will vary.

page 24 (Vegetables Checklist 2)
Answers will vary.

page 25 (Squash—Vegetable or Fruit?)
2. acorn squash = 7 seeds
   pumpkin = 10 seeds
   zucchini = 5 seeds
3. Answers will vary.

page 26 (Traffic Light Peppers)
Check coloring for understanding.

page 27 (Many Kinds of Tomatoes)
2. cherry tomatoes = 5
   grape tomatoes = 10
   Roma tomatoes = 2
   beefsteak tomato = 1
3. Answers will vary.

page 28 (Leaf Vegetables)
2. *Row 1* carrots
   Row 2 green beans

page 29 (Eating Orange Roots!)
1. 6 carrots
2. Answers will vary.

page 30 (Hidden Vegetables)
2 broccoli stalks

page 31 (A Purple Vegetable)
Check the dot-to-dot for accuracy and the tracing.

Answer Key (cont.)

page 32 (Garden Maze)
Possible Maze Solution

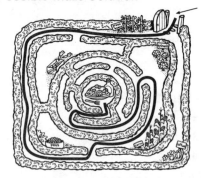

page 33 (Grains Checklist)
Answers will vary.

page 34-35 (The Little Red Hen)
No answer key necessary.

page 36 (Whole Grains—Wheat)
Answers will vary.

page 37 (Whole Grains—Oats)
  1 & 2. Check coloring.
  3. Answers will vary.

page 38 (Whole Grains—Corn)
  1. Check coloring.
  2. Answers will vary.

page 39 (Whole Grains—Barley)
No answer key necessary.

page 40 (Whole Grains—Brown Rice)
Check coloring for understanding.
Colors will vary for bowl.

page 41 (Dairy Checklist)
Answers will vary.

page 42 (Where Does Milk Come From?)
No answer key necessary.

page 43 (Dairy Foods)

Row 1 = broccoli
Row 2 = apple
Row 3 = corn on the cob

page 44 (Find the Dairy Food)

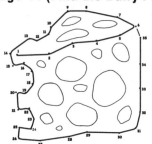

Swiss cheese

page 45 (My Dairy Foods)
Answers will vary.

page 46 (Protein Checklist)
Answers will vary.

page 47 (Protein)
meat, fish, eggs
nuts, seeds, beans

page 48 (Protein Makes Us Strong)
Pictures in each box should be colored.

page 49 (Nuts Are Protein, Too!)
  1. 10 hazelnuts
  2. Check counting and student drawing.

page 50 (Foods of Every Color)
Answers will vary.
  1. strawberries   red
  2. blueberries   blue
  3. plum   purple
  4. wheat bread   brown
  5. corn   yellow
  6. milk   white
  7. lettuce   green
  8. orange   orange

Answer Key *(cont.)*

page 51 (Food Groups)
1. Fruits—apple, banana, cherries, grapes, peach, pear
2. Vegetables—broccoli, lettuce, corn, and celery.

page 52 (More Food Groups)
1. banana
2. bagel
3 wheat bread
4. carrots
5. milk

page 53 (Which Group?)

Note: Cheese is a dairy product but is also a good source of protein. Corn is a vegetable, but when ground up, it is considered a grain!

page 54 (Eat Healthy Foods)
pears, apples
carrots

page 55 (My Favorites)
Answers will vary.

page 56 (Healthy Foods Chart)
fruits = 4
vegetables = 3
grains = 3
protein = 2
dairy = 2

page 57 (Foods to Know)
Answers will vary.
1. asparagus—vegetable (4 sylables)
2. barley—grain (2 sylables)
3. broccoli—vegetable (3 sylables)
4. soybeans (edemame)—soy is a protein-rich vegetable (2 sylables)
5. kiwi fruit—fruit (3 sylables)
6. mango—fruit (2 sylables)
7. oatmeal—grain (2 sylables)
8. yogurt—dairy (2 sylables)

page 58 (Find the Healthy Foods)
Discuss choices with students to determine understanding of the difference between healthy foods and treats or "sometimes" foods.

page 59 (Make Healthy Choices)
1. Answers will vary.
2. Answers will vary.

page 60 (Keep Food Safe)
No answer key necessary.

page 61 (Stay Healthy)

page 62 (Sleep and Rest)

page 63 (Wash Your Hands)
Discuss each picture with students to clarify what each one suggests.
Pictures for boxes: before a meal, when dirty after playing, after petting animals, and after sneezing.

page 64 (What Do You Use?)
Circle the faucet, bar of soap, pump soap, and the towel.

page 65 (If You Are Sick)
Row 1—Cross out the two children sharing a drink.
Row 2—Cross out the boy coughing without covering his mouth with a tissue or his elbow.
Row 3—Cross out the boy rubbing his eyes with dirty hands.

page 66 (Teeth Need Care)
Color 1, 2, 3, 4.

page 67 (Be Safe)
Check each student's page for understanding.

page 68 (Stretch and Move)
No answer key necessary.

page 69 (Moving in Place)
No answer key necessary.

page 70 (Moving Every Day)
1. stretch
2. bend
3. climb
4. squat

page 71 (Healthy Actions)
Answers will vary.

page 72 (Playground Fun)
1. Check that students have drawn lines to the appropriate pictures.
2. Color the jump rope, ball, hula hoop, bicycle, skateboard, and skates.

page 73 (Make Your Own Music)
No answer key necessary.

page 74 (Move to Music)
No answer key necessary.

page 75 (Move Like an Animal)
No answer key necessary.

page 76 (More Animal Moves)
No answer key necessary.

page 77 (Circus Fun)
No answer key necessary.

page 78–79 (Ideas for Outdoors)
No answer key necessary.